JESUS LAW

The Crossroads of Law and Religion

by Reverend Anna Grace

**CreateSpace Independent Publishing Platform, North
Charleston, SC Library of Congress Control Number:
2016906483
KDP**

Table of Contents

Chapter 1: The Foundation of Governmental Systems

The closer one examines the petals of the flower, the further he strays from the root. Though the petals of the rose may be the most attractive and intoxicating portion, intensive focus upon the flora may cause one to miss the thorn in the stem. So it is with the study of world governments. Though we may be distracted by the unique and diverse colors and shapes and sizes of the multitude of legislative systems present in the world, perhaps it's time to consider the dirt they all stem from. The theory I will posit here from an allegorical standpoint is that the "devil" lives in the soils of the systems of all governments. The devil, according to Biblical definition, is the hidden progenitor of the framework of government, and hence there is much pain and suffering inherent within it.

To describe the devil, the King James Authorized Version calls him "the prince of this world" indicating he is the ruler of this earth. If so, he indeed would rule through today's legislative organization, as world governments are the current rulers of this world. To get to the root of the devil's methodology in ruling over this world, we will first need to identify the similarities within the variety of established governments on the earth instead of belaboring their differences. Perhaps if we can identify these deeper threads of consensus within all governments rather than picking apart the cords of contention, we can arrive at a harmonious commonality amongst governing bodies in this world.

Recognizing similar components in all governments may assist in concluding for peace in all nations. Perhaps we can also then discover the defect within the system of government that has allowed for war, oppression and suffering. Perhaps an understanding can be realized to eradicate the biases between governments, their peoples and the multitude of nations if we focus on the congruences. There has always been competition and discord in the proverbial field of flowers. However, revealing how all come from the same ground may be able to have a unifying effect, and we may be able to start fertilizing the soil rather than plundering it.

In fact, I propound that a theoretical cure for the strife between and within various government systems has already been put forth by

Jesus in the Bible. To much dismay, however, few have been able to decipher Jesus' hidden code of legislative ideology. Not many even consider Jesus as a scholar of law and government, though he is prophesied to be a great ruler over all the nations some day.

Though this thesis is meant to be a serious inquiry into Christian law and philosophy, because secular law is deeply entangled with religious law and philosophy also, both systems will be equally weighed. Re*lig*ion itself is a form of law, as the root of the word religion indicates. Through the study of etymology, which is the study of the origin of words, we can discover a link between religion and legislation. '*Lg*' is the root of the word re*lig*ion and also the root of other words, such as *lig*ament , and it means *bands* or *bonds*. The words *leg*al or *legi*slate have the same root as the words religion and ligament '*lg*.' These legal terms are derived from a root which means *to bind fast*. Both re*lig*ion and *leg*al mean to be *bound* by law, a *legal binding*. Religion and Law both speak of a binding covenant between two entities.

A religion, therefore, (as obvious in religions that stem from the Bible) at its base is a set of binding laws that one must adhere to; for in order for a religion to be sovereign, its adherents must abide by a certain set of ordinances and rituals or laws and commands. If the Christian or Jewish religion didn't have a set of rules or standards, it would lose its God. God is the one who gave these nations rules and laws and commandments to follow. Without these defining characters of obedience to law, Christianity or Judaism would not be separate from any other organization.   In fact, all religions, no matter how liberal or conservative, have a set of rules and regulations to set them apart from other factions of worship. One is known as a Muslim, abiding by the Islamic faith, because of his obedience to and observation of the rules of Ramadan, for instance.

In like fashion, a government of a nation has a set of legally binding statutes to adhere to and uphold in order that it maintain its own sovereignty from other nations. Constituents of a nation must obey certain laws and abide within certain *bound*aries in order to be counted as a countryman of that nation. There is that word again "bound", "bind", "band". Humans band together by agreeing to follow a certain set of binding ordinances. In a country, physical boundaries are delineated, but also physical activity is bound by the laws of that land. For example, one is not allowed to run around naked in his community, as that would go outside the boundaries of the law of his community. Both religious groups and nations bind their members by placing boundaries of law around geographic location and/or physical behavior. Each person who belongs to one of these two groups (and all humans are part of a nation) are obligated to obey rules in order to belong and to stay within the nation's borders. So we see that both groups, religious and patriotic, are similar at their foundations, both being run by obedience to a unique set of laws and statutes.

There is more accordance in governments around the world than discrepancy, if we investigate the essential mass, which is always the root. Yes, from fascists to monarchies to republics, world governments all have one thing in common: In order to be a sovereign and separate nation, there are always a set of legally binding laws to adhere to. This seems irrelevant at the surface, but upon deep philosophical analysis, this congruity will turn out to be severely critical. In fact, it is of such crucial consequence, the seemingly overwhelming exterior differences between varying forms of government become invalid to the point of negligibility. In essence, the structure of all governments is based on the same principle.

Again, it (like religion) requires obedience by its subjects to a set of rules and laws, even if a government is found on the basis of complete freedom and liberty. At the foundation, there are always boundaries to adhere to.

So at the beginning, as humankind began to set up civilizations, perhaps (per historical examination) in the area of Ancient Babylon, mankind frames together a set of rules to govern groups of people who desire to live within close proximity with each other. Presumably, these laws dictate certain acceptable social behaviors appropriate for public common areas, laws regarding fair trade among the people, laws regarding treatment of aliens who come into the area, a myriad of punishments for those who break laws, a set of officials to implement law, a set of judges to interpret and legislate these laws, a special group to enforce law, and the conditions go on and on and on. All governments operate under these same basic principles. Of course there are slight variations. For instance, some nations have a one man ruling party, while others rely on a jury of peers to judge, but both systems are still structured very similarly in principle.

There is a story about the implementation of man's constructs for civilization and government depicted allegorically in the Bible.

You may be familiar with the Tower of Babel incident in the very early days of civilization. Here is a brief synopsis from Genesis 11:

"And it came to pass, as they journeyed from the east, that they found a plain in the land of Shinar (the ancient name for the territory later known as Babylonia); and they dwelt there. And they said one to another, Go to, let us make brick, and burn them throughly. And they had brick for stone, and slime had they for morter [sic]. And they said, Go to, let us build us a city and a tower, whose top *may reach* unto heaven; and let us make us a name, lest we be scattered abroad upon the face of the whole earth. And the LORD came down to see the city and the tower, which the children of men builded. And the LORD said, Behold, the people *is* one, and they have all one language; and this they begin to do: and now nothing will be restrained from them, which they have imagined to do. Go to, let us go down, and there confound their language, that they may not understand one another's speech."

The parallel between this story and that of the beginnings of governed civilization may be inconspicuous, but when we analyze this scripture in a future chapter, its analogy to the development of world governments will become obvious. It teaches a profound lesson about the implementation of law in society.

Babel and Babylon stem from the same word in Hebrew, and the correlation is plainly seen even by those who don't study language in the corresponding letters *bbl*. As anthropology has proven the earliest of civilizations to be located in the area of Babylon, so does Babel speak to the formation of a civilized society.

Civilization is predicated by law. If there were no laws or rules or ordinances, there would not be a civilized society. The very definition of "civilized" is that a civilization must be substantiated upon the foundation of obedience to law or government. This very characteristic makes man able to live in a community together. Societies who are bound together by obedience to similar laws and principles then draw bounded or limited areas around these groups who have agreed to follow the same set of laws. Boundaries of cities or nations therefore spring up around groups of people who are following the same set of laws. From the premises of limited areas bound together through legal concord arises the entity of sovereign and separate national governments, arguably the highest form of rulership in the world.

At what degree these supreme governmental systems label themselves on the spectrum of conservatism to liberalism is of little concern. The focus needs to be concentrated at the base once again. The devil is in the fundamental details of this structure, the root of governments. The problem is not in the diversity of flowery and elaborate myriad of varying government systems, but it is in the very principle of government itself. The very foundation of the government ruling system is flawed.

The average person may not believe that his government is a flawed government. He lives peacefully for the most part in his daily life and is happy with the amount of freedom that he has to go about his business in safety and security. Though this may be true, we know also that many are not happy; there is still much crime and discontent. There is hardship, pain, and suffering, and our governments war and squabble with its own populations as well as with other nations to this day.

The flaw in government systems is that they are founded on the principle which dictates this incorrect hypothesis: in order for man to behave in a civilized fashion and in order for man to live in a harmonious society in close contact with other men, laws must be implemented. Read that statement again, and let it sink in. Laws are created based on the assumption that man needs law to behave, belong, be normal, and be safe. Law is given charge over man's behavior and law is responsible for keeping peace. Government is charged with the authority and obligation for upholding, legislating, and enforcing good behavior and keeping men safe within its boundaries by upholding peace.

If this principle proves to be true – that governments are needed to keep men in order and to keep enemies at bay, it leaves individual man with little responsibility. In opposition to this system, we can postulate that man can regulate himself and should be allowed to govern his own behavior. Perhaps it is not the government that needs to be liable for the behavior of men. Perhaps it is the duty rather of the individual man to find goodness and responsibility within himself, rather than rely on an outside authority to tell him by laws and rules what is right and what is wrong. Perhaps the right to author what is right and wrong, lawful and unlawful, or good and evil, has fallen into the wrong hands.

The principles of our government systems today rely on the belief that man needs government to give him laws delineating how to behave, and man also needs government to keep him safe. Law, then, and by proxy government, is that which defines what is good and acceptable behavior for man and his neighbors, and what is bad and unacceptable behavior for man and his neighbors, through legislation. Is it not legislation which reveals to us the knowledge of what is good, safe, acceptable, and holy behavior, and what is evil, unacceptable, harmful, criminal, and unrighteous behavior?

For ages man has pondered the legendary Tree of Knowledge of Good and Evil as found in the Serpent's territory in the Garden of Eden. Contemplate this secret no longer...*Law* is the knowledge of what is good and what is evil. Laws define the very foundation of that which is good and that which is sinful and bad. And government is in charge of law.

Hence, it would quite literally be the serpent, also known as the devil, that is at the foundation of legal systems and the governments that rule over those systems, according to the story of the Tree of Knowledge in Genesis 2 and 3:

"And out of the ground made the LORD God to grow every tree that is pleasant to the sight, and good for food; the tree of life also in the midst of the garden, and the tree of knowledge of good and evil."

"Now the serpent was more subtil than any beast of the field which the LORD God had made. And he said unto the woman, Yea, hath God said, Ye shall not eat of every tree of the garden? And the woman said unto the serpent, We may eat of the fruit of the trees of the garden: But of the fruit of the tree which *is* in the midst of the garden, God hath said, Ye shall not eat of it, neither shall ye touch it, lest ye die. And the serpent said unto the woman, Ye shall not surely die: For God doth know that in the day ye eat thereof, then your eyes shall be opened, and ye shall be as gods, knowing good and evil. And when the woman saw that the tree *was* good for food, and that it *was* pleasant to the eyes, and a tree to be desired to make *one* wise, she took of the fruit thereof, and did eat, and gave also unto her husband with her; and he did eat."

Chapter 2 – The Structure of Legislative and Religious Systems

In the Old Testament, God through Moses set up a system of governance over the Israelites. Thus begins one of the earliest and most comprehensive records of civil legislature. God decreed his ordinances, statutes, and commandments, which included approximately 613 laws, rules, and regulations. At Mount Sinai when presented with these laws, the Israelite community contracted with God in Exodus 19:8, "And all the people answered together, and said, All that the LORD hath spoken we will do. And Moses returned the words of the people unto the LORD." God in turn promised to give the people a land flowing with milk and honey. Hence, the genesis of a historically significant legally binding contract between God and man.

Through this covenant a nation is born, a government is born, and a religion is born. As discussed in the previous chapter, laws are the foundation for each of these systems. Without law, one can not have a sovereign nation. Without law to define the limitations of a religion, one can not have a religion. What makes one religion different from another? The laws and standards which they uphold. One religion observes a holy and sacred day on Saturday. Another religion observes a holy and sacred day on Friday. And yet another one observes their holy day on Sunday. These standards and regulations are that which define the religion itself. These limitations and boundaries are the adhesive glue that hold religious sects together.

Once a legally binding agreement is accepted by joining a religion, for instance, the direct result is a conscious change in behavior and possibly in beliefs in order that the contract of the new religion is upheld. Social adaptations are implemented so that one can live within the boundaries of the limits of the religious laws. And thus, a whole new lifestyle is also born, simply by the practice of agreed upon rules of certain societies and certain religions. Behaving according to the standard of the commandments became a way of life for the Isrealites in the Bible, and everyday their behaviors were intended to uphold their religious requirements; it was not as simple as going to a ceremony on the Sabbath.

Secondly, once there is a legal agreement between a person and their practiced religion to adhere to the religion, a ruling class of lawyers and judges is in place so that the person can be monitored regarding the requirements needed to comply with the law. The Israelites relied on Moses and the High Priest Aaron to help direct the people to be obedient to the statutes ordained in the law. The responsibility of maintaining all 613 commandments became a monumental task for Moses and Aaron, and so priests and judges were assigned to share this responsibility. Moses and Aaron were the "ruling class", the sect of society which has authority over the rules and legislation.

In order to qualify for the position of judge, one needs to know intimately all the practices of social law, and likewise to be a priest, one has to know intimately the practices of religious rite. Suddenly a hierarchy is formed. Now, there were constituents from the bloodline of Levi exclusively (in the example of the Israelites) who were allowed to legislate law, minister unto God, and receive the special benefits and exemptions of the priesthood/government. In choosing a special tribe to ordain law, a royal class is created. Royal means regal and the word regal is directly related to the word regulate and "regulations" – regulations being another word for "laws". Therefore, the existence of regulations demands for a regal and royal court, as the existence of rules always demands a ruling class. This centralized bureaucratic system carries on via the lineage of Levi through many many generations in the case of Judaism.

At the top of this hierarchy of course, is God. Moses sits on the throne just below him. Aaron and the clergy are also in esteemed positions of authority above the laity. To help reinforce the idea of hierarchy, the tabernacle, or central place of religious and legal assembly, is erected where commoners come to worship and to have their disputes heard before the board of judges. However, only certain clean and prepared ministers are allowed into the most sacred areas of the tabernacle, and only the High Priest alone is allowed into the Holy of Holies where it is thought that the presence of God resides. A separation is inherent now between the common unclean population and the specially cleansed and holy royal court.

This Israelite blueprint for the management of legislation is not the first appearance of a hierarchical bureaucracy within societies in history. We have a mountain of evidence which suggests that Egypt, among others, was a civilization based upon the same structure that is being presented above from the Biblical text. A royal bloodline governed the land, headed up by a supreme "God" (Pharaohs were known as gods), from a centralized location, with a basic set of rules and laws, and with various temples and monuments for worship, and rites and rituals for practice. The point proven here is the one we already discussed in the first chapter of this book: Any society that comes together as a united group of persons, is glued together by law, which leads to limits and boundaries of behavior, limits and boundaries of territory, centralized control over others, and a revered and select ruling class to legislate the laws of the land. This fundamental system of government therefore predates the Israelites.

The same framework for law/government is alive and well to this very day. Though civil governments and religions all call themselves by different names, the inherent structure of their governments is a hierarchy of honored bureaucrats, starting from the top with the royal family or High Priest or Pope, or Prime Minister, etc. The members of the ruling class or ministry are next in line, including those with the responsibility of law-making, law-interpreting, and law-enforcing (whether civil or religious law), and lastly the common population. There is no exception within the existing nations or churches of modernity nor ancient history. None deviate very far from this similar framework. In fact, our theory is that neither a sovereign nation nor a sovereign religion can exist without these inherent castes and social orders, for they are what defines bureaucracy.

The Israelite entanglement of government and church was not as unique or novel as one might imagine. One thing we see in the Bible is an outline not only for a legislative and judicial philosophy, but also a set of religious laws which were deeply intertwined with the secular philosophies, statutes, and doctrines. However, most contemporary civilizations of the time were also very devoted to the worship of gods in their daily secular activities, and God was an intricate fundamental piece of the communal and legislative puzzle. The worship of the same deity and the performance of his or her religious requirements was just as much the cement that held societies together as civil laws. Often the religious and civil laws overlapped because one philosophy is similar to the other.

For instance, a certain group of people believes that God has a set of rules that they must live by in order to be blessed or rewarded in life or in the afterlife. This group believes that if God is pleased, things go well. If God is angry, things fall apart. So, written into their very civil structure are laws that agree with God, and cause the people to behave as God would have them behave.

All throughout scripture, the people are warned of mingling with others who worship different gods. Perhaps the God of Israel understood the cohesive effect of religious beliefs and ideologies, and this is indeed why religious law is so deeply enmeshed in the principles of the Israelite civil law. God worship is a uniting factor among societies.

Even in modern day, the constitutional law in the United States is based on the fundamental principles of the God of the Bible. Much of the Western World believes the Bible is a guide or reasonable book of instruction, and through our belief, we accept a set of social, civil, legal, and religious customs and traditions. In fact, there are definitely three major religions in the world today which have a tremendous influence on how their nations operate. But in reality, all governments are somehow related to theology. Any ultimate authority in any nation is mimicking the role of God. The very definition of God is the idea of the highest authority. Government and law is the authority on earth, the God of this world.

The theory here is that people believe God is a ruler, a creator of laws and order, and one who shows favor to a certain class of clean and holy servants. This is exactly why our rulership mirrors this system. Our governments are our gods; they rule and reign over us as God on the earth with ultimate authority.

Many believe in the image of God who is a Judge, for he has given good moral, ethical and physical laws for humanity to live by. God then legislates that law, upholds those laws, and judges by those laws. If he has ordered Moses to structure the Israelite community in this manner, God's paradise must be structured in a similar manner. God had promised the Israelites that if they followed his laws, they would inherit a land flowing with milk and honey. This is the proverbial paradise. One of the basic reasons why these laws are followed is because of the promise that it will result in a harmonious ethical society, where people can live in a peaceful, loving, and beautiful land. God has promised a perfect society for those who follow his laws. God has promised privilege to those who obey and live holy, good, clean lives and privileges for the elect individuals of intimacy with God, absolution, wealth, and favor. These laws therefore must be the way to an idyllic community.

Our governments, hypothetically, make the exact same claim.

God, through his religious ritual, requires a group of faithful servants, those who sacrifice for him, and those who abide by his laws. The contract states that if we serve, sacrifice and obey, we will be blessed and rewarded. Though this God may be called by different names, in the Abrahamic religions, Islam, Judaism, and Christianity, his characteristics are very similar. Through the Bible, what was once a Middle Eastern concept, has now become a Western concept – God rules man by implementing laws. These laws are what God judges mankind by. And so the societies in the countries where these religions are dominant certainly have used their basic beliefs surrounding God and his laws to found their civil structure. Now manmade government structures rule over men by the implementation of laws, and these laws are what the governments judge mankind by.

As we have already shown, there are certainly numerous nations in the world who similarly use Biblical *principles* as a guideline or starting point for their own governmental, legislative, international, or religious systems, picking and choosing (whether wittingly or unwittingly) from the main precepts and ideas of the book as we have already shown. Quite honestly, the Bible is simply describing a system that has been used in all nations over all eras to govern men. The principles are not unique to the Bible, the Bible is just describing the structure of government as it exists already. The Bible covers all legal disciplines so thoroughly, anyone who would endeavor to found a sovereign nation/government would be hard pressed to deviate substantially from foundational Biblical principles. The central fulcrum of the Bible is its idea for the framework for government, and each government today is founded on the very same principle: Man needs rules to keep him in check and these rules will create a harmonious society. This concept is the main concept of the Bible also.

In following this structure, all nations thereby validate at least a nominal belief of some kind of Ultimate Authority, or God, who rules in this way, whether they connect these principles to the Bible or not. Even if they adamantly deny this God of the Bible and his religion, it is true that they still allow their governments to rule in the same exact manner that this God rules over men. They have adopted the same form of government as God has.

In summation, because most nations adhere to the principle structure for government as outlined in the Bible, by proxy they give some credence to and validation to this God. If they truly don't have faith in this God or his blueprint for governing mankind, their government should not follow his principles nor be founded on his same legal structure.

Everything from the rules for strategies of war to the laws regarding the moral treatment of widows can be found within the pages of the Bible. It is one of the most comprehensive documents regarding civil and religious structure and law, and the best selling text ever. To declare that its civil and religious structures don't mingle, and so neither do our modern day governmental laws, is erroneous. To say that the Bible is simply a Holy Book dealing with religion would be outrageously understated. By the same token, to state it is simply a guide for legislative structures is just as understated. Its ideologies seem to have had wide reaching influence on both religious and societal practices in much of the Western (and Middle Eastern) world today, whether consciously or subconsciously, and should not be disregarded.

Fortunately or unfortunately, there has been no alternative to this way of governing men or nations. There has been no other option to structure government in all the anals of history. Though there are dictators, monarchies, tyrants, republics, all exist by the implementation of law to manage behaviors and to manage any threats to their own peaceful nation. Their foundations are all the same.

Chapter 3: The Dichotomy of Law

In a Western society, people are very familiar with at least ten of God's commandments in the Bible. Along with those ten are hundreds of others, from the very broad to the very narrow. Though many nations may be founded on the Bible's principles as far as structure (that man needs to have law in order to live in a peaceful, heavenly, milk and honey society), those same nations certainly don't implement each individual miniscule law outlined in the Bible. Many laws from the Old Testament are today abolished and eradicated all together.

For instance, it would be quite surprising if a church, any church or government, were to take it upon themselves to enforce the law that one can not trim his sideburns or beard in a certain manner. This rule seems not only primitive, but completely impractical and useless. Yet, on the other hand, many churches and governments do still abide by the sentiment of the law which states that homosexuality is an atrocious sin. Still obeyed also is the law, "Do not steal." We therefore adhere to some of the Biblical laws, but not by other Biblical laws. This dichotomy is true for the rest of the 600 plus laws, and so our system seems to be built upon a bit of hypocrisy.

If we believe in the foundational principles of God's governmental and religious structure, namely that man needs a governing authority to tell him what is right and wrong and to keep society in order, why do we shun some of the lesser rules?

If we don't go as far as to follow every detailed law, especially those regarding daily rituals because they are impractical and useless, perhaps the foundation those laws are based upon is also impractical and useless. It was said that following those regulations would result in a society that could exist with harmony, love, and security in paradise-like land. Perhaps we should be more stringent in our adherence to each and every law like the bible teaches, or perhaps we need to wholly abolish them and their foundations all together. As of this point, we are half in and half out.

One thing is certain regarding this dichotomy; living within the midst of obedience to some of the laws and ignorance of the other half of the laws has not delivered us to a smoothly functioning heavenly community as it promised it would. Though all governments and religions are based on similar principles, with promises of protection and peace, the world is still filled with pain and suffering.

Should we possibly take on each and every law with even more gusto and determination to see if we indeed can create a heavenly community in doing so? Or should we abolish the whole of the system by getting rid of all the foundational laws of governing, and more importantly the principles they are based on since we disregard many simple laws every day such as speed limit signs? Or is it indeed lenience and disregard of law that would lead to the demise of civiliation itself?

Fortunately, in history we have an example of a society who strictly adhered to each and every law "religiously" and tried desperately to implement their legal system to the letter in order that they could obtain their promised harmonious community. Let us look at this society from the viewpoint of hindsight, for hindsight is 20/20. Let us do better than that, and let us examine this Jewish society from hindsight **and** by the mouth of the very members of this nation, the New Testament Jews. The New Testament Jews have a lot to discuss when it comes to how the Israelites fared when abiding stringently by all the foundational principles, the tedious laws, and the holy commandments in their Torah (Law).

Let's begin with the most famous Jew of the New Testament, Jesus Christ.

We must admit that even every good Bible-believing Christian doesn't follow each trivial law of old. Perhaps this is because we understand that Jesus came to be the sacrificial lamb for the world, and so at least we can validate the abolition of the law of animal sacrifice, if not many of the other laws through Jesus' death. It is stated that Jesus has satisfied the ritual requirement for blood sacrifice. Let us further investigate what Jesus has accomplished and what Jesus says about following the legally binding laws and ordinances of the Old Testament.

Jesus said in Matt 5:17, "Think not that I am come to destroy the law, or the prophets: I am not come to destroy, but to fulfil." **To fulfill means to satisfy all requirements and obligations.** Accomplish, achieve, complete, realize, meet, answer, fill, end, terminate, conclude. Which laws and requirements did Jesus come to fulfill? Which ordinances and commandments did Jesus come to terminate? Which principles and beliefs did Jesus come to end? Out of the 613 commands, which are the believers of modernity still to abide by and which have been satisfied? The answer should obviously be all of them, but remember, in principle, we still are governed under the exact structures of this biblical system of law and we still implement Old Testament laws like "Do not steal" and "Do not kill."

To pick through the Old Testament to determine which obligations are still necessary and which are concluded by Jesus seems a monumental task. Let's put this in perspective. The Old Testament says in Deuteronomy 19 regarding a criminal act, an eye for an eye and a tooth for a tooth. Does our legal system abide by this law? Yes, when a criminal is named and charged and convicted, he must repay through fines or jail time according to what is deemed to be equivalent to the pain or loss incurred by his crime. Of course, sometimes murder requires the death of the perpetrator, a life for a life. Obviously, Jesus didn't come to satisfy this law, because to this day a life is sometimes taken to pay retribution for a life that was taken.

This portion of the law is still in effect then. If a person were to break a law in the Jewish community, the usual punishment was death, exile, or retribution equal to the loss incurred by the crime. We see a similar legislative structure in our courtrooms today. If a person breaks a rule, he can expect a sentence similar to one of these disciplinary actions – a fine or retribution, exile from society by incarceration, or death. So, the punishments for crime still follow the archetype of Moses' structure. Likewise, this same Old Testament system of criminal activity, trial before the law, and retribution for the crime is followed in many countries today. Assuredly, Jesus didn't mean to terminate this system.

Does our religious structure still require that we serve God as Moses and all of his people did in the Old Testament? Yes, if we are believers, all of us must serve God and do good deeds if we want to be "accounted worthy" (Luke 20:35) to get into heaven. And many religions believe in some kind of service or servitude toward God, so the law of service to God is still valid in religion and often still of value even in secular ideologies. Thus, behaving well according to the standard of law and doing good deeds in the name of God is practiced today. Jesus certainly wouldn't want to end this practice.

We have given two examples of foundational doctrines from the Bible that are still implemented today. What of this law in the Old Testament? Exodus 31:15 states, "Six days may work be done; but in the seventh is the sabbath of rest, holy to the LORD: whosoever doeth any work in the sabbath day, he shall surely be put to death." Do we kill people, or is it even deemed 'illegal' to work on a Saturday? Of course not. Jesus must have fulfilled this requirement. And this, as stated in Leviticus 11:12, "Whatsoever hath no fins nor scales in the waters, that shall be an abomination unto you." This ordinance declares shrimp and lobster need be off our menus. Jesus must have fulfilled this law because we don't obey this one. Exodus 21:17 commands, "And he that curseth his father, or his mother, shall surely be put to death." Luckily, Jesus fulfilled this one or every teenager would be on death row.

Our real life examples above demonstrate that we believe that Jesus has fulfilled some of the laws, but not all of them. Over the millenia, we have determined that some of these rules are just too harsh or too plainly ridiculous. However, the Ten Commandments are religiously taught in Christian churches around the globe, and so are those ten laws still considered efficacious and reasonable?

Now we are presented with an oxymoron. If Jesus was not lying, and he finished, fulfilled, and concluded the law, why is any of it still practiced and why are our foundational structures of society still based upon it? This is an interesting contradiction and seems to present a bit of hypocrisy. Perhaps instead of trying to weed out which laws Jesus satisfied, the better angle would be to investigate *why* Jesus came to fulfill the laws from the Old Testament.

The fundamental principle here which completely escapes Christianity in the Western World is the fact that all of these rules from Jehovah (God) through Moses were holding the Jews to a very restrictive, very tedious, and very laborious set of legally binding requirements. Jesus came to fulfill these old rules, precisely because they were holding the Jewish nation in bondage. Haven't we heard that Jesus came to set the prisoners free?

What was holding the people in captivity? The same thing that holds people in prison today – the law, the legal system, both civil and religious. Under the Biblical principle, one is *bound* to uphold his end of the contract (which is to follow the laws), in order that God uphold his end of the contract (which is to give us peace in the heavenly land).

The Jewish priests and the Jewish community both were striving and toiling in service or servitude to God, desperately trying to accomplish the entirety of the letter of the law down to every miniscule "jot and tittle." All of these requirements consumed their lives, holding them bound by their legal contract with God.

They had agreed in a mutually binding covenant to adhere to every law so that they could inherit a land flowing with milk and honey, and this very law had put them in bondage to accomplish the whole of 613 impossible tasks. New Testament scripture says in Gal 4:24 "...the one [covenant] from the mount Sinai (where God's principles for government were ordained), which gendereth to *bondage*." We already explained in Chapter 1 that law always genders to bondage, for that is the very definition of the word *leg*al, and re*lig*ion - bands that bind.

So Jesus came to set the Jews free from this bondage. Yet, now we, through our legislative system have taken on a similar burden, for we still abide by the foundational principles behind these old rules. The phrase "slave to the system" should come to mind.

Thoroughly more important than the details we have just outlined above is the belief in the foundation of government itself. We still believe that if we obey appropriately and serve faithfully and punish the criminals accordingly, we can earn our place in the Promised Land of a good and peaceful society. We still believe that if we implement laws and a ruling class to legislate and punish criminals, our society can be harmonious and secure, with equality for all. We still believe that man needs government to be responsible for limiting other men's behaviors and for keeping individual men safe and secure from their enemies.

These former statements are simply riddled with falsehood – law inherently separates by creating a ruling class; hierarchy can never accomplish equality. Remember, the very existence of rules demands a ruling class, which is an inequality in men. Government does not need to outline rules for man's behavior as it leaves the man unaccountable for his own moral understanding and growth.

It is a conspicuously incorrect philosophy to continue to believe that following these legal precepts and maintaining our governmental systems according to those precepts is the way to a heavenly community. By example of the Jewish community, the system failed miserably. Following these principles didn't work with the Jewish nation, and it isn't working now in any other nation. We simply don't understand that Jesus actually had come to save us from these very principles and doctrines. Colossians 2:14 states "having spoiled principalities [principles] and powers, he [Jesus] made a shew of them openly, triumphing over them in it." He actually came to triumph over the principles upon which society's legislation operated. Let's continue with more indisputable evidence that Jesus was against the legal systems of his day which were outlined in the Law of Moses.

Not only was the Law holding the Jewish people in captivity through the immensely taxing daily rituals, the principles behind the law were causing the people and judges of the law to be discriminatory. If a person was found to be in noncompliance with the tediously intricate requirements, he was shunned from society or demeaned in the community. The law is what gave the society a basis for judging some as good and others as bad. Their ideology, derived from their legislative principles, revealed that some were indeed somehow degenerate or evil while others were holy, righteous, and special – according to the basis of laws outlined in their scripture. The law, and only the law, cast a negative light on some behaviors, or lack of behaviors, making it possible for discrimination to arise. If a person did not act according to the law, he was not good, not strong, not disciplined, not faithful. This type of labeling creates discrimination which creates more separation and unrest in society, not unifcation and harmony.

Though it reveals what acts and behaviors are good and holy, the law, and only the law, also reveals what is wrong with people, sinful, or evil. It doesn't only reveal what is wrong with others, it **defines** it. If there were no law to break, there would be no concept of criminality in society. Ponder this concept deeply. Romans 4:15 states, "for where no law is, *there is* no transgression." This statement has two meanings. It describes how one can not break a law if there are no laws to break, which is a bit tongue-in-cheek. But the other meaning is much more profound and revelatory: It is the law that **causes** transgression because the foundation for the law is flawed.

Here, the law is described as faulty in scripture in Hebrews 8:7 "For if that first *covenant* had been faultless, then should no place have been sought for the second." Recall the covenant made at Mt.Sinai between Moses, God, and the Isrealites for obedience to God's rules. Thus, the whole system is confused and faulty from the start, as it breeds a belief in an erroneous principle, namely, that man is bad from the get-go, and would go stark wild without the long arm of the law.

There is a long psychological discourse recorded in the chapter of Romans 7 explaining how man is not evil, but only twisted in his thought because of being taught by law that something rather benign is illegal by law. On the other hand, something that is legal may feel rather hostile. To honor and obey some laws, however, one must rise against his own intuition and do as the law suggests, rather than what is in his heart to do. His mind begins to question his idea of benign behavior, and he may begin to doubt his own judgment specifically because society's law defines this seemingly benign behavior as unacceptable and immoral. Perhaps, then it is the man himself who is mistaken, and perhaps his thoughts are not clear. He begins to distrust his own ability to discern right versus wrong. A mind that is thinking correctly does not commit a crime. Unfortunately, the law is responsible for making a man believe he is thinking incorrectly. The logic here suggests that it is only a mind that is confused that can commit a crime. Let's analyze.

Romans 7:9-11 sums up the corruption caused by the governmental and religious system, "For I was alive without the law once: but when the commandment came, sin revived, and I died. And the commandment, which was ordained to life, I found to be unto death. For sin, taking occasion by the commandment, deceived me, and by it slew me." This passage conveys the message that without law, we are free to do as we see fit. However, when the gauntlet of law falls upon us, we are now obliged to restrict our behaviors to remain within the limitations of legal behavior. The writer is not actually slain or dead in the above scripture, but is spiritually dead, psychologically bound to confine his behaviors and his thoughts, even against his own conscience, and rather to work to obey constantly regardless if he believes his obedience is correct. He must limit his own freedom to express himself so that he abide within the boundaries of law. This lack of freedom is described as death in the above verse.

Confusion by the burden of believing in the divisive and discriminatory principles put forth through the law is one side of the coin that is detrimental. To be "deceived" by law in being told that to cut one's sideburns and beard in a certain way is unacceptable and evil, is also very confusing and detrimental, for there literally seems to be no *sane* basis for such vain restrictions. But again, man must not question the law as put forth by the highest authority in the land, so though it may be impractical, men will keep themselves in the long side burn and beard fashion. Man no longer trusts his instincts, which probably says, Hey, who cares the way I wear my sideburns? He now doubts his decision making skills and decides to conform to society's rules and standards. Of course this is one ridiculous example of how the law deceives and allows sin to "take occasion" through law. Man now distrusts himself and practices a ritual which goes against his better judgment, which eventually will "slay" the unique individual spirit of the man, as is what happened to the author of the verses in Romans 7.

There are dozens and dozens of examples of irrelevant restrictions in the 613 rules in Jewish law, including one that restricts one's ability to wear fabric that mixes two types of cloth together, such as wool and cotton, for instance. Some of these rules seem to be benign enough, but there are also rules that deal with serious inquiry into the moral behaviors of man. Unfortunately, the relatively important rules are made marginally impertinent by their relativity to such ridiculously trivial rules. There are hundreds of rules in existence like this in today's society also. Are we to take seriously a rule that states a person can not speed down the highway, when this law stands next to a law that states that a person can not carry an ice cream cone in his back pocket, as dictated by Alabama state law?

God did say back in the Garden, that if Adam and Eve ate of the fruit of the tree with the knowledge of good and evil, they would 'die.'

Adam and Eve did not die physically, they definitely went on to live and procreate Cain and Abel. They were cursed instead to live in a state of spiritual and psychological death by the knowledge of what was good and what was evil. Remember that today, law defines what is good, legal, and acceptable behavior, and also what is evil, illegal, or unacceptable behavior. In essence, the knowledge of laws which define good and evil, puts us in a state of death because we are no longer free to act of our own volition, but must restrict ourselves to live within the boundaries of acceptable laws.

The entire Jewish society was cursed to not only slave and toil to serve God in strict obedience to all of his rules, but also cursed by the false beliefs created through flawed principles. As stated in Romans 7, they were deceived, and Galatians 3:10 states, "For as many as are of the works of the law are under the curse:" Man is not able to rest psychologically from fear of discrimination if he steps outside the laws, but his intuition tells him that some of these laws are excessively trivial and binding. Always overshadowing him is the worry that if he does break the law, he will not be accepted, good, or found worthy. This existence is indeed a curse once one is aware of its futility.

So in the New Testament through Jesus and his disciples, we discover that the system creates bondage, inequality, spiritual death, confusion, and discrimination, NOT the promised beautiful life in a heavenly peaceful community it was supposed to create. The Jewish nation was actually under a curse (which is why they needed a Messiah/Savior). Jesus came to save them from their *laws* and their *religion*.

Is it not so, then, that nations that abide by the foundation principles established through government, are under a similar curse also? The *curse* is described in the Bible as continually striving and toiling in a system that will never put out what it promises to put out. Futility and perpetual enslavement is the curse. Inequality and fear based upon the knowledge of transgression and threat of punishment and exile is the curse. Psychological confusion, insecurity, and spiritual death is the curse. If all this is true, laws and government will never bring us a harmonious society.

This philosophy can bring its students deep into the psychology of fear. With the invention of the doctrine of sin (where something is inherently evil or illegal) and our belief in it, comes the manipulation of the psyche through deception.

This proverbial fall of man will be spoken of in the next chapter.

The Bible says in the New Testament that the only way to make it to heaven is through faith in Christ, yet we still try to abide by the laws of Jehovah (the God of the Old Testament) in order to set up our own heavenly community. We have just proven that adhering to those principles doesn't lead to heaven, but hell. Scripture states that Jesus came here to fulfill those laws, and to triumph over the principles upon which they stood. Roman 10:4 states "For Christ is the end of the law for righteousness" simply because abiding by law will not make a man righteous, but confused instead. Hence, the law needed to be ended, which is why Jesus shows up in the New Testament.

However, in stubbornly continiuing to form our societies on the basis of law and government, we have actually tainted our society with bondage, death, and discrimination. Is there any need to wonder then why there is so much pain and suffering in the world if much of the whole system is structured around principles which are proven in the New Testament to *not* work?

Jesus came to defeat all the old principles and the structures that were built upon those principles. Colossians 2:14-15 states, "Blotting out the handwriting of ordinances that was against us, which was contrary to us, and took it out of the way, nailing it to his cross; *And* having spoiled principalities and powers, he made a shew of them openly, triumphing over them in it."

The truth is Jesus came to fulfill and blot out *all* of these written laws because they were against us. If we put these passages in modern terms, we could say that Jesus came to *delete* the rules of old and to prove the very reason the rules were put in place was irrational in the first place. In effect, none of the laws of the Old Testament need be regarded any longer, but neither does the entire system need to be regarded any longer. Jesus *fulfilled* the law, even the Ten Commandments, unless Jesus was not telling the truth when he said he came to fulfill the law, or failed to accomplish what he said he would do.

The truth is Jesus deleted all of the principles for the need for governing humanity, and the laws which sprung from them, but our society and our churches don't follow that fact and still base their foundational structures and beliefs on ancient frameworks. One might say that though we believe the Bible, we actually have no faith in Christ. This is where our hypocrisy is revealed. Jesus used the word 'Hypocrite' many times in scripture, and it was because man believes that law and government is good, though he lives under its rule in death and enslavement, perpetuating erroneous beliefs and pain and suffering.

Christ came to do away with these religious and legal structures because they, in fact, *don't* lead to a harmonious and peaceful society. We just don't understand that, and we continue to practice law and religion in our reality. We claim we believe in Christ's teachings and follow Christ, but in reality we still believe in the law and its subsequent systems of law enforcement and legislation. Jesus taught us something new, and the reason is because the "devil" was at the root of the law. The enemy that Jesus came to slay at the cross was the Law and all of its ordinances, statutes, and commands which led to the legal and religious structure of his day, which is the same structure in modern day. If the law was the enemy, it follows then that the one who put forth the law was the nemesis of God, our enemy, he who gives the knowledge of good and evil, the devil.

Chapter 4: The Devil Is in the Foundation

Ironically, we have established that the very law that was supposed to bring us into a heavenly existence accomplished the very opposite. We have learned that inherent in the law is the concept of separatism, discrimation, bondage and other atrocities. In order for a nation to be sovereign unto its laws, it also intrinsically must be separated from others who don't quite conform. It not only separates nations, but communities and individuals into castes.

We have learned that the legally binding agreement between God and the whole world (who has followed principles which predate the Bible, but are also detailed in the Bible), has caused enslavement to the system, discrimination by criminalization, spiritual death by futile obedience, and erroneous beliefs. The system has created a bunch of servants, who toil and strive to be good enough for a reward that can not be realized.

Let us analyze the story of the Tower of Babel so that we can see what happened at the foundation of civilization, as purported and perpetuated by the Middle Eastern (Biblical) ideologies. From Genesis 11 again:

"And it came to pass, as they journeyed from the east, that they found a plain in the land of Shinar; and dwelt there." Shinar is defined in the Hebrew Concordance as the ancient name for the territory later known as Babylonia. Babylonia today is located in Mesopotamia, the land that is roughly referred to as the Middle East today. The Biblical concepts that we adhere to today derive from the area of Babylon. Babylon is the land of Jewish captivity and bondage, for they were enslaved by the Babylonian government for 70 years. The King of Babylon in Isaiah 14 is named Lucifer. Perhaps then it was Lucifer who understood the deep effect that religious worship has upon a nation, and so introduced religious principles into civil legislation. In this way, all the world could worship him. Whatever is derived from Babylon must be from Lucifer, as he is the King of Babylon. It is no coincidence that the word *Bible* and the word *Babel/Babylon* stem from the same root. If you have ever wondered what the word Bible could possibly mean, now you know: A book of binding law from Babel/Babylon.

"And they said one to another, Go to, let us make brick, and burn them throughly. And they had brick for stone, and slime had they for morter [sic]." Bricks are not the preferred building material in the Bible. Repeatedly the contrast of unhewn stone is pitted against the concept of hewn stone, or fashioned brick, in scripture. Bricks demonstrate the concept of uniformity, where unhewn stones are unique and diverse. Bricks are all the same color, shape, and size. The laws presented in Babylon demanded conformity. One was not allowed to express his individual size or shape, for he was limited by the confines of law. Law requires that all will behave within the same regulations, law requires that all obey the same hierarchical structure, law requires all to believe in the same acceptable ideals, law requires that all wear their hair and beards the same in some societies. This is the definition of uniformity, conformity with the result being like-minded molded "bricks". If one steps outside those boundaries by being unique, he is breaking social and religious custom, and deserves punishment and/or discrimination.

Conformity as opposed to diversity assures one of a boring life in hell, where humanity is not allowed to grow or blossom or expand into unique "unhewn" individuals. The glue which holds these bricks together is slime. Its cohesive ability is in question, and in the long run, slime will not do what it is intended to do. Though trying to emphasize and hold on to their commonality with each other through uniformity, the true cohesion is in their differences. What binds the human race is that none of us is the same, and so there is no pressure to conform to any form of normalcy or perfection. Diversity dismisses the pressure to be perfect, for perfect and dull normalcy can not exist where the foundation is uniqueness.

"And they said, Go to, let us build us a city and a tower, whose top may reach unto heaven; and let us make us a name, lest we be scattered abroad upon the face of the whole earth." So the people try to construct their own system to reach a heavenly society. The framework they are using to build this structure is one of conformity and dubious cohesion. We have just described how basing our civilization on conformity by law does not unify, but separates. It does not cause peace but discord. It does not create harmony, but discrimination. Thus, heaven can not be obtained.

"And the LORD came down to see the city and the tower, which the children of men builded. And the LORD said, Behold, the people *is* one, and they have all one language; and this they begin to do: and now nothing will be restrained from them, which they have imagined to do. Go to, let us go down, and there confound their language, that they may not understand one another's speech." The people of the world have agreed to structure all governments and all societies on planet Earth in the same governing way. This has been detrimental to their psyche however, rather than beneficial. Their sense of self is confused by the limitations of having manipulated their own individuality to conform like bricks to laws. One language the people have now, the language of Babel. Babel and Babylon both mean 'confusion' in the Hebrew tongue. Confusion is their language, "babble" in the English language. For they had laid the foundation for a society which they thought would bring them to heavenly peace and harmony, but instead would lead to death and bondage. And none would be able to get to the root of the problem, for that devil is a very subtle deceiver. In truth, it is the pride of humanity who thought that he could create his own system to have his own heaven, which has led to the fall of civilization.

Law causes *spiritual death*. This form of government/religion is not the way to God. And, yes, even Christianity, whether they admit it or not, still practices the same system of commandments, service, sacrifice, tithing, priesthoods, etc. as put forth by Moses. They have not yet seen the light of Christ's ways.

As the New Testament criticism of law begins to take shape in one's mind, the truth becomes obvious and can not be denied. If this governmental structure does not work, The God of the Old Testament who outlined a system for us, that was contrary to us, against us, causing death, bondage, enslavement, discrimination, and separatism, is not a good God. How could this be God at all? It was none other but that subtle serpent, wrapped around that tree of knowledge of good and evil. It is his system of law, and this system alone, that gave humanity the knowledge of what is supposedly good, and what is supposedly evil by the standard of government. The tree of knowledge of good and evil is the foundation of societal structure of law and government, and thus all that is evident in those that abide by this structure is disharmony and suffering. An evil tree cannot bring forth good fruit, and we have all eaten of this same tree.

The Bible, which is the book of the law, even defines itself as the knowledge of good and evil. It is written in Deuteronomy 30:10, 15: "If thou shalt hearken unto the voice of the LORD thy God, to keep his commandments and his statutes which are written in <u>this book of the law</u>

[the Torah/Bible]...See, I have set before thee this day [in this book of the law] life and *good*, and death and *evil*;" The book of the law was the forbidden fruit in the garden, the fruit from the tree of knowledge of good and evil. It is known that the act of eating from this tree caused the "fall" of man, which is simply a confused state of psyche. In essence, we still reside in the beautiful garden of Eden, called Mother Earth, we just can't see it nor can we attain its peace due to the proverbial curse given after Adam and Eve ate of the tree.

The allegorical enemy has us believing that these systems of legislation will work for us. Laws are the answer for peace in our society, and religious practices will lead us to intimacy with God in his holy land. But we have already tried this for millennia; neither works. It was a deception.

There is simply proof upon proof upon proof that the God of the Old Testament principles is the nemesis of the True God. Though the information is hidden deeply within the doctrines of the scriptures, once a person knows what to look for, the evidence can not be denied. For those who are not convinced that the serpent (the devil) has hidden behind the name of God

Jehovah for all these eons, here are some of the scriptures that should make you think again:

1.) Was Jesus YHVH's son?

    a) Jesus was vehemently opposed to the law of YHVH and Moses. One of Jesus' accomplishments at the cross was to delete the ordinances and laws of the old covenant as stated in Colossians 2:14, " Blotting out the handwriting of ordinances that was against us, which was contrary to us, and took it out of the way, nailing it to his cross."

    b) Though Jesus seems to advise the law abiding man in Matthew 19 and Luke 18 to follow the commandments in order to secure eternal life, Jesus ends these parables with a riddle. He essentially says to the man that it is not sufficient that this man has kept every single commandment since the man was young. Jesus says, You yet lackest. Jesus declares that this man still falls short because the law is not the way to God.

    c) Jesus is the end of the law for those who believe, Romans 10:4. Why is Jesus the end of his own father's law? Why did Jesus break the stoning rule of the law when he encountered the crowd who was condemning the adulterous woman? Why was Jesus considered an outlaw by the Jewish population who worshipped the God of the law? Why does the New Testament never mention the name Jehovah? Why did Jesus tell the worshippers of the law and Moses that their father is the devil in John 8, but he called his own father God?

2.) Why does Moses (God's messenger) wield a *Serpent* Staff of Power?

Exodus 4:2-4 says, "And the LORD said unto him, What is that in thine hand? And he said, A rod. And he said, Cast it on the ground. And he cast it on the ground, and it became a serpent; and Moses fled from before it. And the LORD said unto Moses, Put forth thine hand, and take it by the tail. And he put forth his hand, and caught it, and it became a rod in his hand:"

Moses, the receiver of the law on Mt. Sinai was bestowed all of his power from his infamous staff. The staff was able to bring the plagues of Egypt and turn the River Nile into blood. The staff needed to be held up when the Israelites were fighting the Amorites in the desert, for when he put the staff down, the Amorites surged and would begin to win over Israel. The staff was a

Serpent. The power of the mighty staff was of the serpent, the devil. A wooden staff which is also a serpent is the same symbol as the symbol of the serpent on the Tree of Knowledge.

3.) Why is God called Satan Twice in Scripture?

a) Numbers 22:22 - And God's anger was kindled because he went: and the angel of the LORD stood in the way for an adversary** (Hebrew word *satan*) against him.

b) 2 Sam 24:1 & 1 Chronicles 21:1 both record the one and only census that King David took of Israel. However, it seems to be described as David having been instructed to take this cense by the Lord by Sanuel's account, and by Satan in the Chronicle of the account. "And again the anger of the LORD was kindled against Israel, and he moved David against them to say, Go, number Israel and Judah." And in Chronicles 21, "And Satan stood up against Israel, and provoked David to number Israel."

Satan and God are not distinguished in the Old Testament. They are one in the same. Isaiah 45:7 says, "I form the light and create darkness: I make peace and create evil: I the Lord do all these things." Remember, scripture also says in Matthew 7:18, "A good tree cannot bring forth evil fruit, neither can a corrupt tree bring forth good fruit." So this entity here in Isaiah can not be good if he is creating evil. This surely sounds like good and evil mixed here. And we know that it is the serpent who deceives by good and evil doctrines from Babylon, the land of confusion.

4.) Moses – Hero or Villain?

It is strange that revered Moses, whom Christianity continues to worship as a hero, played the role of the administrator of the law, if the law was indeed from the devil. But have you ever seen ancient paintings or sculptures of Moses? Maybe this is why he was depicted in this manner several times in historical art. Here are true pictures of real live sculptures of Moses for your review, and there are dozens of these similar depictions of him on this planet.

These sculptures might not prove anything significant on their own. But when we start to put the pieces of the puzzle together, it means that his character was a little shady at the very least.

The Bible itself confirms that these images are historically correct. Exodus 34:29 says, "And it came to pass, when Moses came down from Mount Sinai with the two tables of testimony in Moses' hand, when he came down from the mount, Moses wist not that the skin of his face **shone*** while he talked with him." According to Strong's Concordance H7160 (shone*) means:
to shine

1. (Qal) to send out rays
2. (Hiphil) to display or grow horns, be horned

'To shine, to send out rays,' is the first definition, and definition number two is 'to grow horns, to be horned.' So, yes, it does seem that Moses' face could have grown horns, according to scripture. This should indicate 'devil' to us, should it not?

5.) God the Destroyer?

In speaking about the same group of people that the Lord led out of Egypt, 1 Corinthians 10 says, "Moreover, brethren, I would not that ye should be ignorant, how that all our fathers were under the cloud, and all passed through the sea; And were all baptized unto Moses in the cloud and in the sea; ...But with many of them God was not well pleased: for they were overthrown in the wilderness....Neither murmur ye, as some of them also murmured, and were destroyed of *the destroyer*."

Now was it the Destroyer who destroyed these people as stated above, or was it the Lord who destroyed them as stated in Jude? Jude 1:5 says, "I will therefore put you in remembrance, though ye once knew this, how that *the Lord*, having saved the people out of the land of Egypt, afterward destroyed them that believed not."

Revelation 9:11 describes this destroyer again, "And they had a king over them, which is *the angel of the bottomless pit* [Lucifer over hell], whose name in the Hebrew tongue is Abaddon, but in the Greek tongue hath his name *Apollyon*." The exact definition of the word Apollyon in the

Greek Strong's Concordance is "Destroyer." For those who know Hebrew, you also see the character of Abaddon described in his name. The first part of the word, Aba, is a transliteration of the word Abba, meaning Father. Don means judge in Hebrew. Abaddon means Father the Judge. We now know that the judge, the highest administrator in the court of Law, is the angel over the bottomless pit, the Destroyer, Satan himself. Isn't is supposed to be the God of the Law who judges? And again, was it the Lord or the Destroyer who destroyed the people? It seems they are one in the same.

6.) Horrific Scriptures

This is why we see multiple verses like this in the bible: Numbers 31:17-18 where "God" orders, "Now therefore kill every male among the little ones, and kill every woman that hath known man by lying with him. But all the women children, that have not known a man by lying with him, keep alive for yourselves." One does note here that the Lord is telling them to take female children for the purpose of lying with them. Hosea 13:16 allows for the killing of infants, "Samaria shall become desolate; for she hath rebelled against her God: they shall fall by the sword: their infants shall be dashed in pieces, and their women with child shall be ripped up." There are so many verses where the Lord YHVH, Jehovah, Yahweh, God, speaks despicably in regard to concubines, slaves, the murder of children, and slaughter of all kinds. If we wanted to list them, we would need a separate novel. The truth, however, is that it is the character of Lucifer demanding all of these things, hiding behind the name of God.

In essence, the world, then, is left following the concepts, principles, doctrines, and beliefs put forth by the proverbial enemy, Lucifer. These concepts do not work, nor do the structures built upon them. This is why Jesus came to save us from this God and his law.

There is simply such a tremendous amount of literature to support this theory within the very pages of the Bible, that it is a complete and utter mystery how those who have studied this text for decades can continue to be ignorant of this fact. I can not judge, as it took me five years to decode the mystery and decipher the riddle. Indoctrination is a very difficult thing to overcome.

7.) Generation of Vipers

One final piece of evidence for this book, though there are several others in scripture: Jesus called the very religious, very dedicated, very faithful law-abiding priests and judges of the Jewish nation vipers and serpents. He said to those who were strictly following Jehovah's law in John 8:44, "Ye are of your father the devil, and the lusts of your father ye will do. He was a murderer from the beginning, and abode not in the truth, because there is no truth in him. When he speaketh a lie, he speaketh of his own: for he is a liar, and the father of it." Please take note again that this was spoken by Jesus to the priests and ministers and judges of the Old Testament Law as translated by Moses. It's not as if these devout men switched allegiance wittingly in their years of sacrifice, servitude, and piety - it's that they were following the wrong entity all along, deceived by what they thought was good, but actually turned out to be evil.

Jesus came to reveal the truth, the way, and the life. If Jesus came with the truth to the Jewish nation, what were the Jews practicing before Jesus? A lie. If Jesus came to bring the way to heaven, what were the Jews practicing before Jesus came? A false promise for heaven. If Jesus was life, the Jews of his time were still practicing death. Jesus revealed a different God who didn't promise something he couldn't deliver. Jesus reveals a new system which actually sets us on the path to a heavenly community, and a better covenant with life instead of the "covenant of death" (Isaiah 28:15) from the O.T. Jesus came to bring freedom and liberty through truth, instead of captivity and death by falsehood.

8.) The Devil is Destroyed?

It is ironic that the one faction of peoples on planet Earth that believes in the devil are the Christians. If you ask an atheist or Buddhist or even a Jew if they believe in the devil, you'd be hard pressed to get an affirmative answer. Christians, however, believe in the devil whole-heartedly. This is dangerous territory though because Jesus's main purpose for coming to earth was to destroy the devil.

1 John 3:8, "For this purpose the Son of God was manifested, that he might destroy the works of the devil."

Hebrews 2:14 "Forasmuch then as the children are partakers of flesh and blood, he also himself likewise took part in the same; that through death he might destroy him that had the power of death, that is, the devil."

Hence, it seems as if Christianity does not believe that Jesus accomplished what he came to earth to do, destroy the devil and blot out the laws at the cross. They very much believe Satan is alive and well deceiving many individuals causing them to sin. They also very much believe in many of the laws of the old covenant. Jesus had two accomplishments on earth, ending the law and bringing a new covenant, and destroying the devil. One would have to imagine the both were the enemy of Christ. The devil and the law were the enemies of Christ because the law was given by the devil.

Chapter 5: Jesus' Law

    If what is purported in the previous chapters is true, according to Jesus we are now left without a civil and religious structure, for the old foundational laws and the principles upon which they stood are supposed to be done away with by his death at the cross. Contrastingly, and perhaps unfortunately, our systems today still uphold many of the foundational beliefs of the Old Testament. Jesus, as we have discovered, actually came to blot out that governing system of law. Jesus Christ was at odds (to put it mildly) with the religious system, and was put to death by the civil system of his day, which is still in place in society today. Neither the government system nor the religious system was agreeable to the teachings of Christ.

    Jesus was a radical thinker who went against the governing systems of the day, which were based on the foundational systems of ancient governments and religions. He fought with the leaders of the Jewish religion, and he, again, was put to death by the legal system of the Romans. Granted, the Romans did not have the Jewish laws and texts, but their legislative system was based on the exact same premises as described in the Old Testament law, *as all governing systems are to this day*.

So, we are left questioning what kind of system Jesus proposes for our civilization. What was it that Jesus was suggesting if he was adamantly against the political and religious structures of the day which modeled Old Testament principles? If carnal laws and rules and regulations from misguided doctrines put us into physical bondage, mental confusion, and spiritual death, how is one supposed to be governed and kept in check in modern society? If carnal laws only reveal the sinful nature of criminals, making them always outcast degenerates, how can we change these systems? If we want to be set free from our servitude and obedience to futile conformist principles, let us examine what Jesus came to reveal about law and the governing of mankind.

Though what will be presented here seems idealistic, the greatest minds who ever lived have agreed with what Jesus teaches. Please understand that few have understood this hidden wisdom within Jesus' system, and understand that no nation in the world has followed Jesus' ideas up until this point. It is yet to be seen if Jesus' philosophy would bring about the Promised Utopia. The only thing we can surmise is that, as demonstrated throughout history and up until modern times, the ancient and Old Testament mimicking systems have not brought forth a harmonious society.

To begin to comprehend the new ruling system, which is called *spiritual law* and *new covenant* in the New Testament, a summary of the incident in John 8 will be analyzed:

"They say unto him [Jesus], Master, this woman was taken in adultery, in the very act. Now Moses in the law commanded us, that such should be stoned: but what sayest thou? So when they continued asking him, he lifted up himself, and said unto them, He that is without sin among you, let him first cast a stone at her. And they which heard it,   being convicted by *their own conscience*, went out one by one, beginning at the eldest, even unto the last: and Jesus was left alone, and the woman standing in the midst. When Jesus had lifted up himself, and saw none but the woman, he said unto her, Woman, where are those thine accusers? hath no man condemned thee? She said, No man, Lord. And Jesus said unto her, Neither do I condemn thee:"

Though the old carnal law of Moses demanded that the people stone this woman to death (and our social system today still condemns this act of adultery at least by ridicule or mockery or shame or discrimination), Jesus proposed something new. Jesus knew that all of those participating in this public berating had also committed sin, as sin is defined only by law and all were under law. In asking the first perfect man to pick up the first stone, he knew that this woman could be set free. She would not be condemned to death. She would be forgiven and given back her life.

When Jesus so carefully presented by default the fact that all could theoretically be stoned because not one had been without sin, their conscience convicted them. Here is the turning point in our understanding. This group of peers felt guilty, convicted by their *conscience* that they were about to commit a heinous act of murder according to their law. They realized suddenly that the law had told them to do something evil. Their conscience, on the other hand, was telling them the truth – "It is wrong to harm another human being, and I am not perfect either, so let me get out of here and leave her alone" said their conscience hypothetically.

The law therefore had lied to them in trying to convey a morally decent way to deal with this situation. To stone is not morally decent, said their conscience. To punish is not morally decent, said their conscience. Their law had deceived them into thinking it was okay to harm another because the person had committed a sin. Fortunately, their conscience was the victor in the fight of morality. Their conscience knew it was wrong to harm another, even though their laws and commandments demanded her stoning in order to correct the wrong that had been committed; and so they left. The conscience instead said do no harm, in essence – forgive.

When we know what to look for, we begin to see this truth all over the scripture. **It is our heart and our conscience which tells us the truth of right and wrong, morality and immorality, ethical practices versus unethical practices, good and evil, not the principles found in the law of commandments.** Romans 2:14-15 says, "For when the Gentiles, which have not the law, do *by nature* the things contained in the law, these, having not the law, are a law unto themselves: Which shew the work of the law written in their *hearts*, their *conscience* also bearing witness." Again, the summation of these verses tells us that the truth of what is morally just is already written in the hearts and conscience of mankind by our Maker. This law which is written in our hearts *by nature* is called the spiritual law. Law is written into our moral compass of right and wrong, not on a piece of paper (or tables of stone for that matter) in a court of law.

If you truly had to pick up a stone and kill your child for cursing you out as was required by the law of the Old Testament God, could you do it? Of course not, because your conscience knows this is unjust, and your heart speaks of the love for your child along with your capacity for kindness, forgiveness, and compassion. In this way, our hearts and conscience were meant to be the authority on ethical correctness.

Though most of Christianity believes that Jesus followed the law of Moses, they don't understand that Jesus went beyond the law of Moses into the spiritual law. The example above from John is a perfect criminal court case where Jesus went beyond the letter of the law, and actually *broke* the old precept regarding punishment for adultery. The true judge within him ruled to forgive her because the reality of stoning does not set the stage for a harmonious existence.

Jesus also said in Luke 6:29, "And unto him that smiteth thee on the one cheek offer also the other; and him that taketh away thy cloke forbid not to take thy coat also." Do you see the difference in Jesus? Instead of punishment for the crime against the law which states "thou shalt not steal", Jesus said *let him steal and give him your coat also*. This is completely different from the Old Testament system which deemed that a punishment would be necessary for theft. A new legal system is presented here by Jesus where the heart judges. If the thief needs a cloke desperately enough that he would steal for it, help him out and give him your coat also. Do not seek restitution or punishment, but have mercy.

Jesus was also accused of breaking the Sabbath day law, which is Commandment #4. When Jesus answered those of the Jewish nation who were accusing him of working on the Sabbath, Jesus recounted that their very own King David broke a law by eating the holy shewbread which was set aside for the priests only. Jesus said that even their own King had broken the Sabbath day law also. Jesus was simply saying, "Does God really care if you eat bread when you are hungry, when there are literally dozens of loaves to feed the priests who were very well nourished already? Wouldn't it be better to give in charity to one who was starving?" Jesus is prompting the people to think critically, and to show that the truth of the matter is in the heart.

If King David were instead stealing the bread from a poor beggar and her child who had not eaten in two weeks, this might be deemed morally incorrect, and our heart tells us such. However, our conscience also says the law simply doesn't make sense regarding not allowing anyone else to eat the priest's shewbread, for there was plenty to share, in fact often an abundance of excess, so why not share with one who was in need. Why, then, should it be illegal for a starving person to eat the priest's holy shewbread?

Therefore, the law does not have precedence when it comes to judging a person's behavior. Is David bad because he ate the shewbread? He broke a law, but the law was flawed, not David's intentions. Jesus broke the Sabbath by healing a man's hand. Healing was considered work, and no work was to be done on the Sabbath. Jesus answered, "And he said unto them, What man shall there be among you, that shall have one sheep, and if it fall into a pit on the sabbath day, will he not lay hold on it, and lift *it* out?" Here again, the ethical thing to do is help the animal, and therefore in this case, the law to do no work on the Sabbath is not the highest ethical decision. The conscience and the heart take precedence over the written laws.

Of course, the concept that our heart knows better than the court of law seems ridiculously idealistic to most. However, if you analyze and contemplate the scriptures quoted above, you will see that this, indeed, is truth.

Here is the pinnacle of truth in scripture, which we have already touched on. Romans 4:15 expresses a profound and novel idea when it says, "for where no law is, there is no transgression." Thus, having no written law means there can be no criminals, no crime, no sin. For if there is no law to break, there can be no crime committed. It is the law that twists the mind into listening to another outside authority instead of listening to one's own conscience, thereby allowing for one to commit a crime. Only a mind that is twisted will commit a crime and the mind is twisted by babble and immoral laws. If left to his own natural thinking, a person who witnesses a starving person pick up a crumb from another's persons bread loaf will rejoice that the starving man found some nourishment, not slap him in the face for stealing.

In order to believe in the principle that our conscience guides us into correct behavior, and that this conscience is the ultimate and truest governing system inside a man's heart, one would have to believe that there is a light of goodness that lighteth every human who cometh into the world without bias, John 1:9. The Bible teaches that there is a light of life inside of every man.

This light is the light of Christ, and therefore, this living light is inherently pure, good, and loving.

This means that all men and women are *inherently good* in their hearts, for God has literally written truth and goodness and love in the very fiber of the makeup of the human being. God's signature within every man is literally the life energy that animates each individual living human being. That signature is always loving, always filled with light, for that is the very essence of what God is (1 John 1:5, 1 John 4:8). John 1:9 says of Jesus and every man on earth, "*That* was the true Light [Jesus], which lighteth every man that cometh into the world." Every human therefore is good at his core as all have the light of Christ within.

The law, in opposition to this inherent goodness, allows for the belief that man is inherently evil, and if left without a government system ruling over him, he would act immorally, with harm and violence against others. The foundational basis of external governing systems is that humans *need* to be governed because they can not be trusted to behave appropriately with kindness and love.

The foundational basis of the internal intuitive governing system inside the human suggests on the other hand that man is inherently good and has, at the outset, the innocence and purity and goodness of a child. Therefore, if left to follow his own inner authority, his inner voice, he would always do that which is good.

What allows mankind the propensity to misbehave then is the fact that mankind follows corrupted existential laws which twist a man to act *against* his very nature. For instance, according to Old Testament law, a father or mother would have to stone their child for cursing at them. That very signature which God Almighty programmed into man's conscience has to then be denied. In going against their conscience which of course tells them not to harm their child, they instead perform an evil act by listening to their law against cursing, which demands stoning as punishment. It is simply not true that wickedness was their nature, but that they were manipulated by their law to believe they were doing the right thing. This is an extreme example in our day, but consider living in that world just a few centuries ago. Regardless, the principle remains the same. Laws teach us to do incorrectly and to behave incorrectly, no matter how good the law may appear on the surface. Once again the foundational idea of governing law is corrupt, so results only in corruption.

The foundational truth here is that mankind is created in the image of God, and therefore fueled by the very energy of God, which is always good. Even the word God has the same etymology with the word good, for the definition of God is that which is good. This goodness and moral decency is there within every man by nature, for all are made of the essence of God. We are his children. Therefore, mankind can rule himself (if the court system were dethroned as the highest authority on morality), for he knows inherently what is right and wrong.

The existence of evil then is due to the obedience to a contorted governing system, which allows one to hold false beliefs. One can only become evil by a twisting of his own mind to go against his nature. We have been manipulated into believing in evil by allowing a governing law to tell us what is right and wrong. That existential law now becomes the highest authority in the land, the God of the land. But that existential law can never be as fair and just and the voice inside our conscience. Remember, where no law is, there is no transgression. Where law is, there is always transgression and room to judge one as guilty, sinful, evil.

We believe, according to the principles behind our legal systems, in transgression, wrong-doing, sins, criminals, and evil, so now it is substantiated. If mankind is inherently good as he was made in the image of God/goodness and everything was "very good" in the garden, why is there pain and suffering now in this world? What the New Testament proposes is that we erroneously believe in evil, and so it is substance. Through our belief, it is substantiated. Hebrews 11:1 states, "Now faith is the substance of things hoped for, the evidence of things not seen." We have put our faith in a corrupt system and now it has substantiated corruption.

For instance, if a man is homosexual, but he is told this very natural inclination within him is wrong because the law says it is an abomination, he becomes confused, feels anxiety, fear, depression, and inferiority. He wonders why he has this feeling within him, but is not allowed to act upon it because this existential law forbids it. He now must manipulate and suppress his natural feelings in order to fit into society. This pain and suffering is imposed upon him by a false judgment of society, not God. His psyche is now twisted and oppressed, believing he is bad for having these instincts. **It is this type of twisted thinking *only* that can lead to glitches in behavior.** If left to his own nature without judgment from a corrupt law, man is naturally *good*. And this is where the cookie crumbles.

The instant we are told that homosexuality is wrong by a society who is listening to the residual principles of an ancient rule which dictates against it (even though the idea of this should have been erased by Christ), we begin to seek justice against this homosexual behavior and the person committing this crime. The foundational belief is wrong. There is no need to change or condemn or judge the homosexual. God made him perfectly, giving him light in his heart. Where the law makes one believe that he is indeed evil, the truth makes one believe in good. The more who believe in mankind's inherent goodness, no matter his sexual orientation, the more good will materialize, for faith in it is substance, evidence of that which we hope for.

Chapter 6: Equality and Love vs. Hierarchy and Fear

Let's put Jesus' Natural Law to the test by comparing two laws in the Bible. One law says in Leviticus 20:13, "If a man also lie with mankind, as he lieth with a woman, both of them have committed an abomination: they shall surely be put to death; their blood *shall be* upon them." This says homosexuals deserve to be put to death. The other law in Exodus 20:13 says, "Thou shalt not kill."

Both of these acts at one time were deemed evil, sinful, and wrong. Enter Jesus. Jesus has now erased these two existential carnal laws. Where no law is, there is no transgression. So are both murder and homosexuality deemed legally acceptable behaviors now because Jesus has come to end both of these laws against them? This is what we will examine. Are both murder and homosexuality now morally acceptable behaviors because both are now legal? The litigation begins...

Jesus' theory says that mankind knows what is lawful and moral and ethical through the conscience that was given to the human by God himself. This conscience is above and beyond the boundaries of governmental or religious law. Also, man was made perfectly in the image of God without flaw.

With Jesus' philosophy, it is declared that a homosexual person is perfectly made to be homosexual. In keeping with that same doctrine, one might want to argue then that a murderer was created perfectly to be a murderer. Not true. One is different from the other. Here is the explanation.

What is revealed in this philosophy is that mankind is inherently good and perfect. If he or she has done something that our *heart* and *conscience* tell us is morally incorrect, like murder, the conscience reigns and so must be right. Murder is wrong. A man or woman does not commit murder because he or she is naturally wicked and evil, however, for he was created perfectly. However, he or she has committed an immoral act of murder because his or her naturally pure and perfect conscience was contorted, manipulated, or damaged by existential circumstances, beliefs, principles, judgments, and fears. It is only a twisted psyche that can bring forth negative expressions of behavior.

Acts of evil then arise through fear and confusion and false beliefs. To state the obvious, a person committing a crime isn't thinking clearly. Remember our premise, the laws that remain today cause conformity through behavioral adaptation, which is a manipulation of a person's nature. Also, the laws that we abide by today are founded on false beliefs, which is a manipulation of a person's mind. He is no longer thinking *naturally*, and so crime becomes a possible thought.

We have established that the murderer is not evil, just ignorant or confused and thus, behaving wickedly. In the same way, of course, the homosexual is not evil, but still possibly may be confused in the mind. How do we know if being homosexual is something natural or if his or her psyche has also been twisted, and so homosexuality is actually a glitch in behavior caused by a damaged psyche? Now we need to determine if the *act* of murder is inherently wrong as most believe, and if the *act* of homosexuality itself is inherently wrong as many believe.

Let's evaluate what our consciousness says about homosexuality and/or murder remaining in a perfect world where no one is manipulated or twisted by incorrect beliefs. Pretend that Jesus had simply blotted out the pre-programmed opinion in your mind about homosexuality and murder, both of which were probably planted there by the remnants of societal beliefs which are aligned with Old Testament principles. Jesus has whited out what was written by the scripture, which was embraced by society, and grew into a monstrous discriminatory practice. Erase that notion, and believe that God has not decreed a judgment on homosexuality or murder either way. This is how we use our moral compass to determine which act if either, homosexuality or homicide, is morally acceptable:

Ask yourself, are homosexuals harming anyone by committing consensual homosexual acts? Are they creating hate or generating love? Is love of any kind a demonstration of darkness and wickedness, or a demonstration of light and goodness?

The truth that is revealed in my conscience today is that homosexuality is love. Love wins and is eternal, because love is the essence of God. On the other hand, murder does not remain in a perfect heavenly society, because murder harms. The law of the heart dictates that an act of murder is harmful. Death, hate, fear, and harm do not follow us into the Promised Land because they are against God/goodness and harmony and love. Death is done away with but love, consensual love of any kind, remains in our Perfect Society Land.

And so we have easily been able to make a clear, true, pure decision about the law of homosexuality and the law of murder through trust in our very own hearts and conscience. Homosexuality equals love. It harms no one when it is consensual and true. Homosexuality then can remain in the heavenly community because love is our nature. Murder harms and equals darkness and can not remain in the perfect community because harm is against our nature.

Does discrimination of any kind remain in a heavenly society? No, discrimination harms and can not remain in a harmonious civilization. That means all carnal laws that create discrimination have to go. Love is the only law here, for this is where the heart reigns. At its core, the heart can not know discrimination, but only love, for that is the only thing written in it at its core where God lives.

One might also argue that someone's conscience might say something different than another person's conscience. Maybe you think your conscience says that homosexuality is not love, but an abomination. Not so. The beautiful thing about Jesus' theory is that the same truth that was programmed into my conscience before my birth was programmed in your conscience before your birth by the one and only Creator. Therefore, our opinions can not vary (if we wipe away all preconceived notions) on what is acceptable and what is not. That same light and truth that is written in me by nature is written in you, because you and I are made of the same living energy (which is the essence of God.) It's consciousness. If you are conscious, as am I, that consciousness is the living thread which connects all of us on the same communication line with God. Conscience is the great I Am, and all of us have it. It does not vary, but is the absolute truth.

The universe is only made of one substance, *living energy.* Living energy is the actual God of this universe, and so every atom declares the same story and the same truth. The living energy is always only for giving out, sharing, expanding and perpetuating energy. It is a fountain of never-ending abundance and supply and the force within is the essence of light and love only.

To find the original and pure truth that was programmed within us through our own life energy, humanity has to erase all of our preconceived principles that we were indoctrinated throughout many centuries to believe. One must go within oneself, for that is where the kingdom of heaven is found. We must examine our souls, our hearts, and look for that light and that love that we are given by our Creator.

One might also argue that men and women would run wild if there were no laws to control them. Not so, for they are inherently good. If there are no prejudices, fears of judgment, and anxieties about the possibility of misbehaving, then our true essence shines through. When a person is thinking correctly, all that is exhibited is love and goodness and kindness. If no one assumes another is a criminal because there are no laws to judge by, then love and peace begin to reign. Where mistrust was once the base, trust now becomes the foundation. Romans 5:13 states, "For until the law sin was in the world: but sin is not imputed when there is no law." Things change when man's conscience and man's heart is the authority on what is right and what is wrong, and not law. There is now no crime when man trusts himself and others.

When there is no discrimination because the foundational law which supports discrimination is erased, people can love all equally. If one truly, truly loves his neighbor as himself, he would not commit any crime. Fear of any kind can then disappear. Not only are there no punishments, but no one rises above their heart to commit a crime, because heart is the ultimate authority. This is why the Bible in the New Testament says, "For Christ *is* the **end of the law** for righteousness to every one that believeth."

The same holds true for the concept of hierarchies. If no one is deemed better or more holy or more righteous than another because there are no laws to be able to master or laws to fail by, all are equal. The hierarchy of government is not the truth of the heavenly "kingdom". Having more than one caste, or level, in society is diabolical, which means 'of the devil.' Take a look at the Greek word, diabolos from which we get our English word, diabolical. Dia means two, bolos means to cast. To have two castes or more is diabolical, of the devil. And so a government which inherently creates a ruling class and a lay class is flawed.

A parable in scripture is decoded like this: Jesus is called "King of Kings." In a place where all peoples are Kings, who is left to rule over? In a place where all are "raised up to sit in thrones as brothers", says Jesus, who is left to serve the ruling class? No one. Jesus said his kingdom is not of this world, and he meant that it is not structured as we structure our bureaucracies today. In his world, everyone is King and so able to rule over themselves. Unity and equality without conformity are the foundations of this perfect society, unlike the separatism that is caused by the implementation of law.

This concept is also alluded to in Genesis 1 where God gave Adam dominion over all things on earth. Adam, a mere mortal, was supposed to rule, not a God or hierarchy of the elite and entitled. According to the light of Jesus, God is within every human, so men can rule over themselves without an external centralized government.

In order to arrive at a higher wisdom and greater consciousness and to know decisively and purely without bias what our hearts say, we would need to get rid of irrational notions as decreed by legal and civil dogmas and start with love and goodness as our foundation. In this case, the fact that government exists precludes the inherent evil of its subjects and the idea that the nations that surround it are also an evil threat. There is no other reason for its existence. Now, believing in the opposite, we would be able to eliminate the need for a system to tell us how to behave, and with the elimination of the system goes the existence of crime.

We must get rid of prejudice and accept all situations, races, colors, creeds, and orientations. Prejudice is a word that has the same root as the word judgment. Without law, there no longer exists the need for a judge or prejudice. We must focus our hearts upon love, for that is what God is and he embodies the highest wisdom. Then, the truth becomes apparent.

Our entire foundational civil structure would begin to be reshaped, following after a change in beliefs. Humanity's unique differences and unique preferences are demonstrated in our reality to teach us to love all without conditions or rules, not to condemn and hate others for expressing their individual and beautiful qualities.

In the end, it is prophesied there will be peace on earth. This is only achieved if we accept all peoples unconditionally, isn't it so? Then, when there is no basis for people to feel inferior, degenerate, or hated because of conditions placed upon them by societal laws and customs, they are free to live in peace. When there is no basis for other people to feel superior, divine, special, or righteous because they maintain a perfectly holy lifestyle and ostracize the unclean according to a system of law, all can live equally. There is no need any longer to force people into limited conformity, for God himself has chosen to allow for wonderful diversity, lest the world be a dull and uniform hell. And laws do force us instead into bricks of all the same shape, size, and behavior.

In summation, once our belief systems change and once existential laws are eradicated, maliciousness, anger, hostility, pain, suffering, inferiority, and oppression disappear. The Bible says it is principles we fight against, not flesh and blood. Believing the principles of the truth will set us all free. Liberty to the prisoners of law. The system of acceptance through the heart instead of discrimination by law allows for beautiful diversity. Diversity gains us wisdom and teaches us unconditional love, and so we grow closer to godliness.